Eat Your Way
Out of Debt

Jessica Cassidy CNHP CHS

Peak Balanced Health Consulting LLC

This book is dedicated with love to God, my husband, Jon, and my children, Jonathan and Jesslynn. Without their guidance, encouragement and motivation, this book wouldn't exist.

Acknowledgments

This book would not have been possible without the help and continued support from my friend and Editor, Kathy Loo from Kathy Loo VA Services (kathyloova@gmail.com). Her dedication to quality work and her careful guidance is second to none. Thank you, Kathy, for your hard work and wonderful services.

"Thank you, Sandra Durrance for your devotion to the illustration of the cover and also being a devoted and dedicated friend. You friendship continues to bless me and without your encouragement, push and motivation, I would have never finished writing this book. Thank you."

Contents

What People are Saying About "Eating Your Way Out of Debt"

"Jessica's plan is phenomenal. Not only has it helped us move towards a healthier diet, but it also saved us a tremendous amount of money. I spend less on a family of five than I did with a family of four when I didn't know this plan. Who would have thought something so simple could be life changing in so many ways? I highly recommend this book and Jessica's services. If saving your money is a top priority for you, then "Eat Your Way Out of Debt" is a must-have!"–Sandy D.

"Our family wanted to start implementing ideas from Good, Better, Best immediately. We are a large family in debt and we slimmed down everywhere we possibly could. Our monthly grocery bill was more than our mortgage bill and is about equal to our monthly rent. The first thing we started to do was freezer stocking. We decided we would choose one meal a month to focus on, alternating between breakfast and dinner meals. We attempt to use sale items as much as we can and use healthy fillers to make things stretch. Just coming out of a holiday season, we were even able to buy 54 lbs. of turkeys around Christmas for less than the one I purchased at Thanksgiving. There are lots of broth and meals in our future. Thanks Jessica for the wonderful tools you are sharing with families to help them eat their way out of debt."–Kathy L.

Before we used Jessica's system of "Good, Better and Best", we would spend an upwards of roughly $600 a month for a family of five. After implementing her tools, we now spend less than $100a month. Her income tax refund plan has seriously saved us from the paycheck to paycheck mentality. It has given us relief and we eat well every single day and night." — Jason and Hannah A.

"Through the concepts covered in Jessica's class I learned to portion differently and more effectively for my health, and I also learned how to use and reuse every bit of a meal."–Roze S.

Connect with Jessica

Contact Jessica for natural health consultations, or to speak at your next event

FB -Peak Balanced Health Consulting, LLC.
E-Mail -peakbalancedhealth@gmail.com
Web Site - www.peakbalancedhealth.com
Be sure to check back with us frequently and see what is new on our site.

Coming Soon:

*video courses showing how the methods are implemented
*curriculum for commercial venues and Natural Health
  Practitioners

*recipes to keep you on track and within your budget limits
* helpful tips to keep you encouraged
*updates on new publications

Introduction

L ook at our society and you will find a culture that is busting at the seams. We live in a culture where we suffer from "Oh, shiny!!" disease and give into wants and desires to have something right now. In exchange for our wants, is the debt that needs to be paid with a nice little bow wrapped around it called "interest." It costs us more to have something when we desire it immediately versus patiently waiting. The latest smartphones are flaunted in our faces. Better and more luxurious vehicles glisten at the dealership as you drive on by.

Our need for more has seriously taken control over our lives. It isn't just materialism that robs us of our contentment, it is our food too. We gorge ourselves on unhealthy, processed foods and buy into the latest craze assuming it is healthy for us and entrust our government officials to know what is best for us. The average American spends between $500 to $1000 per month on groceries. Some may even argue if that is even enough. More and more people are living paycheck to paycheck as the debt ratio rises and busts the "button" off of your budget.

What if you could eat healthier and save money while doing it? What if there was a way to manage time in such a way where your freezers and pantry are stocked all while saving you time? We live in a fast-paced world and our time is precious. Who wants to spend hours daily preparing meals and prepping? As much as I love cooking, even I cannot do this daily. With life's demands of homeschooling my children, attending school myself, cleaning, handling finances, being active in my community, and chauffeuring my kids around to and from activities, there is absolutely no way I can do it all and do it well without some creativity along the way.

I invite you on a journey with me into the trenches where we will unmask all the facade we see day to day and we will embrace how to live more on quite a bit less. The road less traveled by the American society can lead you onto a pathway of freedom, sustainability and control back into your lives. My hope is that this journey will spark a desire deep in your heart to take the reins from all the marketing gimmicks and make quality food at a fraction of the cost.

Chapter 1
Marketing and How They Lure You In

I's the latest craze! Things like "more fiber", "gluten-free", and "sugar-free" are staples on grocery store shelves. Some products even promote weight loss, promising you the world with a purchase. We have been brainwashed to accept that these products are "healthy" based off of their marketing g immicks. That is exactly what they are–gimmicks. They are out to fill their pockets all while you fill out those jeans you were trying to rid yourself of for a smaller size. Ever wonder why on earth America is grossly obese with all these health claims on the boxes of our food? A bit confused? Let me break it down for you...

If there is a new "study" that arises and gives us an astonishing discovery, you can bet your savings that the marketing industry will devise a plan to make their product appear to align with the study. They don't want to lose your b usiness. After all, if you realize that their food fails to produce the results you are hoping for, these companies would truly suffer, or would t hey? The truth is, the grocery store is not filled with a thousand different companies. It is filled with roughly 10 companies that have bought out other companies and now they own those particular labels. What you are seeing is, in fact, a monopoly of the food supply. he illusion is, we can purchase a better quality product by switching brands, but the reality is, it isn't always the case. Unless you are well-versed on reading nutrition fact labels, and have studied the industry well, it can be very confusing to say the least.

Aren't we getting any nutrition from these foods? If we spend so much on food to be healthy, how come we are one of the most obese nations? This is because the majority of the food is void of true nutrition. Our bodies are intended to have natural/organic foods. It recognizes the DNA from those foods such as: meats, fruits, vegetables, grains, seeds, nuts, milk, cheese, yogurt, eggs etc. Unfortunately, that fiber bar slips by the radar and slows down our digestive process in utter confusion. Our bodies were designed to eat whole foods.

Most Americans live a fast-paced life and the industry targets those that are "on-the-go". That is why there are so many pre-packaged, instant, individually wrapped food-like substances on the grocery store shelves. Who has time to cook anymore? The truth is, we ALL do. Our ancestors worked long hours each day to provide for their families. Sometimes all they would be able to prepare were biscuits, but they made what they had on hand. Nowadays, it is fast food living, or a ready-made lasagna meal to throw in the oven for the family due to lack of time. What are we rushing for? Have we traded values, sitting around the table as a family, for the new "Betty Crocker" promise of all food made in less than 30 minutes? We are worth more than fast and easy.

Our health and wallet need to be taken back from the industry and for us to get back to our roots. We deserve healthy, nutritious foods, and at a fraction of the cost. We can take back the reins of our financial burdens by first starting at the grocery store. Why there? Why the grocery store? It is where most Americans spend a fortune to feed their families–and because of food choices–will spend most of their money later on illnesses. My hope is to help you save money here, teaching you how to properly provide for your family on a budget while changing the dynamic of your eating style. Trust me, when you see the results, you won't be able to go back to spending more for less food. We eat well, every single day. So can you! You know that wonderful saying from St. Jerome, "Good, Better, Best, never let it rest, until your good is better and your better is best"? That is how I operate. I can't even imagine going to the store to purchase organic foods from meat to produce and everything in between without having some tools in my tool belt stashed away to help curb those outrageous costs. Unless you want to take out a second mortgage on your home to be able to eat the best of the best.

I advise you to stay with me and hear these words: No one can start there and save money. I realize that this may sound ironic and a bit certifiably crazy coming from a holistic natural health practitioner who inspires others to eat healthy and balanced meals. You caught me. I totally have a motive and here it is: I want you all to lay down the brownies and ice cream. I want you all to be self-sustainable. I want you to find relief from your ailments and support your systems well, ALL while saving money. I want you to be free of food addictions and to finally LIVE. If that's a crime, lock me up, Sherriff.

What I am about to teach you is a "Good" diet. It incorporates all that you need to have in your tool belt to inspire a lifelong journey into savings and health. It removes the processed foods concept and teaches you to make your foods homemade. This plan is a starting point. Every race has a beginning point and you have to pace yourself to get to the finish line. We all want to win, we all want to be healthy and we all want to enjoy the life we live. What this plan doesn't teach is any other "buzz" words you may have heard such as: organic, vegan, paleo, diabetic cooking, non-GMO foods, antibiotic-free or hormone free dairy and meats. I know, I know. You are so pumped and ready to run that race that you feel you are ready to venture out into unknown territory without your compass for direction. The result of this? A diet that starts out well, but ends in disaster and often encompasses a repeat of past behaviors. So, slow down there, Scooter. This isn't a race where you need to finish first. This is a race where you need to finish well.

Chapter 2
Meal Planning: Not Just for Chefs Anymore

How can we save money if we first do not have a plan? Meal planning is absolutely crucial to your new saving strategy. You wouldn't go out to the battlefield without a strategy of how to win unscathed and you cannot go into the battlefield of the luring products if you plan to stay on a budget without a similar strategy.

I tend to make a menu for the month right before the beginning of the month begins. This is where I decide what we will have for breakfast, lunch, dinner and snacks. All must be included because if you get hungry while you are out and about, the temptation to stop and pick up a quick bite is easier than you think. We must become great planners to prevent us from spending more than we can truly afford on foods that aren't worth the price we pay for them!

There are some points to consider when you wish to meal plan. First, I would always advise taking an inventory of what you already have in the house. You can do it visually, or you can literally write each thing down (this is what I do). There are free planners on the internet that allow you to plug in your ingredients in your pantry, freezers and fridge and will provide you with recipes that accommodate those ingredients. One app that you may wish to look into is "Food Planner". It takes a kitchen inventory, allows you to find recipes on the internet and save them, and you can import your favorite recipes as well. There are many other apps or sites you can use if you choose. I have done this for so long, I don't use anything, but a pad of paper and a pen. Call me old-fashioned!

Once you have jotted down your inventory from your kitchen, it is a great idea to look at the sales of your local grocery stores and see where you can find the best deals. There are times I go to multiple stores to get the best sales and best quality of food for my family. We have a King Soopers (owned by Kroger) that is local and we love the 10/$10 specials. We also have memberships to Sam's Club and Costco that have helped us to save big. We do have access to the military commissary, however there have been many times I have found better deals elsewhere.

When I meal plan, I imagine a plate made of 4 parts before me. A great example of this is from www.choosemyplate.gov. This may seem so commonplace for many of you, but you would be surprised as to how your shopping trip can be detoured by the bright packaging of these foods and bring you away from the simplicity of what our bodies really need. The five components of a plate consist of meat, vegetables, fruit, starch and dairy. Wait! Where are the gra-nola bars, pop pastries, and Chocolate Puffs breakfast cereal? What about cookies, chips, pretzels and crackers? I always despise being the "bad" cop, but alas, it is crucial to arrest the culprits that are disguised as food. C'mon unlawful snacks, it's time to go "down-town".

Another way to seriously save those hard-earned dollars is to find 7 meals your family loves for breakfast, lunch and dinner. When you decide to meal plan, those ingredients from the 7 meals are multiplied by the amount of weeks in the month. The only things you purchase are for those meals in the month. For example, every Monday may be Meatless Chili and everyuesday would beacouesday and so on and so forth! Just when you thought it couldn't get any easier, it just did, because I am about to save you tremendous amounts of time in the kitchen for those busy nights you take the kids to activities or have to work late.

The first week of the month is your cooking week. On Monday, you will make 4-5 weeks worth of chili and rice and freeze the other portions for later weeks. On Tuesday, you are going to make a huge batch of taco meat for every Tuesday of the month, so essentially, you are cooking for one week instead of 4! Your time is just as precious as your health and wallet, and this gives you the opportunity to savor those moments as a family without slave-driving in the kitchen. There are days when we are just too exhausted to whip a meal and this method takes care of this. All of the busy families that work full-time, take the kids to activities, and still have to cook? I hear you and sympathize. This is a way you can accommodate all of those necessary "to-do's" while still saving time and money. If it doesn't speak to either your wallet or your time, it won't be something you will stick to.

Another point to consider when meal planning is the amount of ingredients that are going into your foods. The more ingredients you need to prepare a meal, the more expensive your grocery bill will be. When you begin this journey, I would advise you to use 6 ingredients or less in each meal. In addition to this, I would also use the same type of ingredients that can be incorporated into other meals as well. For example, if you have ham steaks on hand, they go perfectly in breakfast burritos, quiche, macaroni and cheese, soups, hashbrown casseroles etc. Why purchase an additional meat when your ham steaks can definitely make multiple meals for you and your family? Stretch that meat as far as it can go!

Chapter 3
The Set-up: How to Navigate the Store

L OOK at the perimeter of your store. It is literally set up as a square with most of your nutritious foods lining the perimeter, while the bulk of the unhealthy, processed foods line the middle shelves. Produce, meat, dairy, and some frozen vegetables and fruits are great choices on a budget. Are you supposed to forsake all the food in the middle aisles? Absolutely not! There you can find whole wheat pasta, couscous, quinoa, rice, dried beans, corn meal, oatmeal and grits! Those are foods that are loaded with nutrients to keep your body running smoothly and on some high-octane! When we focus on finding meats, starches, vegetables, fruits and dairy of some sorts as the plate from the USDA states, we can ensure that our basic needs are getting met.

Items such as jam, peanut butter, condiments, salad dressing, ketchup, pasta sauce, refried beans and more are there for easy availability, but what they don't want you to know and learn is that you can make all of this and more from the comforts of your own home and the food will taste better and be of better quality than what they provide at the store. It also saves you so much more money all while you are eating REAL foods.

By learning how to make your favorite items at home, it teaches you the skills to provide for your family when the going gets tough in life. You become aware of what is truly in your foods and how to incorporate what you already have at home to make the items you would spend $2 on up for. You worked hard for your paycheck, don't hand it to someone else who wants to sell you a product for less quality than you can make yourself.

If you stroll along the frozen aisles, it is filled with foods that appeal to your sense of eyesight and taste. As we look at the frozen burritos that boast their inexpensive price tag, our mouths salivate at the deal and we place it in our cart...you know, for those late-night snacks. Is it really a deal though? They are often laden with chemicals and preservatives that wreak havoc on your body over time.

Maybe the question should be: Can you afford to be out of work because you have a debilitating disorder that leaves you disabled? You can make your own tortillas for literally pennies on the dollar and if you purchased dried pinto beans, you can make a lot more burritos for way cheaper than what you could purchase at the store. How about those pizzas on pizza nights? Who doesn't love pizza and wing night, especially when watching football? Purchasing from the store versus purchasing from a pizza chain for delivery does save you money, but does it save you the MOST money? No, it does not.

You can make your own dough (or even store bought would suffice if you are not up for the challenge), make your own sauce from tomato sauce, grate your mozzarella cheese and add your favorite toppings for a price that everyone can agree with. What is so great about these types of foods? The burritos and the pizza can both be prepared ahead of time and frozen until you are ready to cook them. For the burritos, I wrap them in foil and reheat in the oven. For the pizza, I stack them 3-high separated with wax paper. If you have a FoodSaver®, you are welcome to use that instead of freezer bags. Now your convenient luxury foods just got even simpler! It is all about what is important to you. We all make time for what is truly important to us, and if health is not your motivation, then let it be your wallet.

Chapter 4
The Battle Rages On: Fresh, Canned or Frozen

WE hear the media and all the nutritional hippies of our day rant on about how nutritious our produce is and how we need to eat more fruits and vegetables. I can't argue (as I have already disclosed I am a holistic health practitioner). This is the complete truth. The average American does not eat enough fiber-rich foods, let alone foods loaded with vitamins and minerals with a wonderful balance of fresh enzymes. I am all for people picking up an apple versus a cupcake any day, but let me show you how to navigate fresh produce when you are on a tight budget.

Unless you purchase only local produce, most of our fruits and vegetables have been shipped all across the U.S. and from other countries. They are usually picked prior to being ripe and then sprayed with chemicals for them to appear ripe and beautiful when they make it to your store shelves. By the time it makes it to your grocery store, it has lost so much of its nutrients, I would call it highway robbery! How do we alleviate this problem if we don't purchase locally grown foods? It is quite simple.

You purchase the least expensive produce on the shelves that are nutrient-dense and the rest will be purchased frozen. Frozen foods are picked at peak ripeness and flash-frozen. Although they do not contain enzymes, they do contain vitamins and minerals and often much cheaper than their "fresh" counterparts. Here is a list of foods I purchase fresh: apples, bananas, celery, lettuce/salad, carrots, potatoes (white, sweet, or fingerlings), onions, greens, beets (be sure to keep the tops as they can be sauteed with spinach and are great to support the liver), mushrooms, rutabaga, acorn squash, butternut squash, spaghetti squash, parsnips etc. Do you see a pattern here? They are predominantly root vegetables that are the least expensive. Expensive items are purchased in the freezer section to keep costs low. I don't believe that one should live on frozen fruits and vegetables alone. The enzymes in our fresh food are vital for our health and it can pose many health concerns if one attempted to just purchase frozen only (let alone canned goods. Please put the can down, walk away to never return).

The idea is to find the, often, overlooked vegetables that hold the most nutrition and are wallet-friendly when fresh. For an added benefit, try to keep as much as you can raw because when nutritious foods are heated, much of the nutrition can cook away. Here are some examples to help: carrots can be sliced or cut into sticks right before eating (the longer they sit after being cut, the less nutrition it holds due to the enzymes breaking down), the beet tops can be chopped into your salad, mushrooms can be sliced into your salad as well. Onions, apples, bananas, and celery all can be eaten raw with no issues. The rest should be cooked for palatability.

You can use frozen vegetables in other ways other than as a dull side as well. You can puree them and turn them into soups for a weeknight meal. A great way to do this is to cook your vegetables and then puree them in a food processor with a bit of chicken or vegetable broth, add your favorite spices and place back in the pot to cook and marinate the flavors. You can add them to your smoothies to give a boost of nutrition. I tend to do this for my daughter since she is totally on the anti-veggie movement, much to my disappointment. You add your fruit, yogurt, milk and sweetener (I use local and raw honey) and about 1/4 cup of frozen peas, spinach, carrots, or kale to the blender and drink away! I would pair all frozen fruits and vegetables with a fresh one to be sure you are getting enough natural enzymes into your diet.

You can also use frozen vegetables to add nutrition to your baked goods (brownies, cakes etc) or use frozen fruit to make your jams, jellies, smoothies, juice, or to make an "ice cream". To make an ice cream, I place frozen sliced bananas into a blender, add just enough milk to the blender to help it to blend nicely and the consistency will be like soft-serve ice cream. It is sweet by itself and can be paired with a homemade strawberry sauce if you choose to make one. You can also dehydrate the fruit for a quick and nutritious snack for the kids. Frozen fruits and vegetables are very versatile and great to have on hand to whip up something delicious in the kitchen in a pinch.

Notice that canned foods are never mentioned to purchase, even the organic kind. Canned goods from the store hold little to no nutrition. Why pay someone to package your favorite vegetable and void it of all nutrition? Does it make sense to place your hard-earned money into the trash and let the garbage man put it in his big, dirty truck for you to never see it again? Of course not! Then why would you purchase canned goods from the store that are doing virtually the same exact thing? Put your money to work where you will get the most nutrition. Fresh is best, and frozen makes runner-up. I realize that many people purchase canned goods from the store in the event of an emergency. If your power goes out, you can't rely on the fresh or the frozen produce because you would have no way to cook them properly. If this is something that really motivates you to purchase canned, learn how to safely can your vegetables at home. Home canning does not void all nutrition from the vegetables and fruits, so you are saving money, building emergency stock for that potential winter storm or natural disaster, and getting nutrition along with it. A great pressure cooker that sits on the stove (I have a Presto) is a great idea. It is a water bath canner and a pressure cooker/canner all in one for less than $70. There are many other varieties as well and some that are even electric! You have to find what is best in your budget and does multiple jobs for the price. Please keep in mind that one must not eat canned foods as their main staple if one wants to remain healthy.

Chapter 5
To Meat or Not to Meat, That is the Question

WE all know that meat is the most expensive part of your grocery bill. It can take your budget soaring over what you can manage very quickly if one is not careful. According to Dr. M. Ted Morter, in his book "Your Health, Your Choice", the average Ameri-can gets too much protein in their diet and it is one of the leading causes of osteoporosis in our nation. Protein is very acidic and as intelligent as our bodies are, it desperately attempts to counteract by alkalizing and buffering the body. What does it use? Calcium!So, it pulls from our bones to balance our bodies, leaving us with less density and more problems.

I am not stating that one should never purchase meat. I am a proud meat-lover who believes in natural B-12 found only in the animal kingdom. I just simply believe in balance and if one consumes the meat, one should also consider that there is protein in all living things including broccoli, spinach, kale, potatoes, quinoa and everything in between.

We have been programmed to believe that protein only comes in the form of meat that has sacrificially died for you to consume. That couldn't be further from the t ruth! Protein is essential to all living things, but one thing you must consider, lest you believe I am leading you down the path of veganism, not all the essential amino acids that we desperately need are found in one place in the plant kingdom. If you are being led to become a vegan, you must master the art of pairing your foods properly to receive all essential nutrients that your body depends on. If you don't want to do all the guesswork, simply put beef, chicken, fish, or pork into your diet. Voila! It's done with the added essential nutrient, B-12!

With all the buzzing of new fad diets, the latest craze is higher protein. That seems to be the key that unlocks all the magical knowledge about nutrition and can prevent disease, right? You want to know what prevents disease? Balance. That is what keeps you afloat in this life and keeps you strong, healthy and vibrant.

Since so many people are hypnotized to think that one should eat an entire chicken or steak for one meal, let me show you the financial benefit of how to break down your meats effectively to save money and to save on health.

A whole chicken can be purchased for less than $7. If you make it the star of the meal, of course you won't have much for leftovers and can find it very expensive. For my family of four we boil the chicken down for a couple of hours in a large pot and take the meat off the bone once it is cooled. We make sure we leave not a shred of meat on the bone and clean the carcass well. We shred the meat and separate the meat into 3 freezer bags (you can vacuum seal if you have a FoodSaver®) and now I have 3 meals plus the bones for me to freeze for later use to make additional broth. I know what some of you might be thinking. "That simply is not enough meat for our family to consume for one meal." Yes, it is when you pair it with other nutritional fillers. One bag of chicken can be made into chicken tacos. I add salsa, homemade refried beans, lettuce, onions, tomatoes, shredded cheese and olives to be paired on the side, along with a whole wheat tortilla. You can add some home-made Spanish rice on the side, corn or sliced avocado to complete the meal. That is plenty of food!

Another idea for the chicken in bag number 2 is to make barbe-cue chicken sandwiches paired with homemade baked fries with steamed vegetables. Bag number 3 can be chicken spaghetti and can be added to a sauce rich in mushrooms, shredded carrots, onions, peppers and tomatoes. This is how you stretch your meat. If you are a family that is larger than our 4, please adjust this to your family's needs, but still use the method of stretching your meat by using vegetables.

We use half a pound of ground beef for a large pot of chili, goulash, soups, or a casserole. Once we put all the vegetables and beans in the chili, serve it with brown rice or cornbread, it is one complete meal. If I am making vegetable beef soup, I am loading the broth with a variety of vegetables and some barley, so the meat ratio can be less. Of course, if you wish to make the occasional meatloaf or burgers, you will need more meat to complete the recipe. In our home, it is a rare occasion when the meat is the star of the meal, so we keep this very limited to keep our costs down.

Pork is often cheaper than beef or chicken and can really stretch. It is one of the most acidic meats and it laden with saturated fat, but on a budget, there are some ways to cut down on the unhealthy fat content when preparing this type of meat. I recommend cooking an entire Boston Butt or Pork shoulder in the oven with water and universal spices such as garlic and pepper on a low temperature until cooked through. Once it is done, remove the pork, shred the meat and place in a colander. Run it through the hot water in your sink to rinse off any fat or grease that may be lingering. You can dry your meat with a towel (paper or cloth) to remove any water from the meat. A large pork shoulder or Boston Butt can generally give us 10 meals each. I separate them in freezer bags labeled with their contents and date and use them in a variety of recipes, such as: bbq pork, enchiladas, shepherd's pie, taco casseroles, or save even more cash by dicing the shredded meat and putting it into soups or make wontons! This meat is not just for barbecue anymore!

If you own a meat grinder, it will pay for itself very quickly. For those of you who own a KitchenAid® mixer, you can purchase the attachments for it instead of purchasing an additional kitchen appliance. I personally have my own meat grinder that is electric instead of manual. What benefit would you obtain from having one of these? Have you seen the prices of ground beef, turkey, chicken and the like at the store? Now, compare your larger cuts of meat and when they are on sale, you purchase those and grind it yourself. You purchase that large 20-pound turkey for $19.00 and then cut pieces of raw meat off and run it through your grinder. You will get more for your money doing it this way, than purchasing it already ground up for you.

What if you don't have the money to purchase a grinder? No worries! I didn't have a grinder for many years and did fine without it. When money was non-existent in our home, I would cook the meat and then run the cooked meat through my little, mini food-processor and make "ground" meat. It is generally drier than meat you cook in a skillet, but is excellent for homemade enchiladas or tacos. It is delicious when paired with onions, peppers, seasonings and cheese. It goes so much further this way and I do recommend that you at least try this as a way to keep costs low. It is one of those methods that should be on every tool belt for those times of need.

There are some days that I dream of silver platters and candle-lit dinners with a fresh bouquet of flowers on my dinner table. Of course, to complete this imagery would be a fine piece of lamb, bison, filet mignon, veal or the like. Due to me being on a budget, it just simply cannot be....right? Wrong! To be honest, a few times a year, we splurge when we see a wonderful sale. I never pay full price for these items and strategically glance at the sell by date when I go shopping. When I see that the date is nearing, I will go to the store and stock up on it when it is reduced due to not selling in enough time. I get amazing deals on terrific cuts of meat that are delicious when I scope out the reduced meats. Sometimes the quality of life is just as important. You don't want to feel like you are in prison and can't eat the foods you love the most. You want to be wise about the way you purchase it and prepare it.

Fish is a terrific alternative to its meat counterparts. It is a lean protein that can also be very cost-effective. After all I have heard and read on Tilapia, I avoid it like the plague, but found Wild Pollock to be just as cost-effective and to be similar in flavor. I can get Wild Pollock fillets for $5 for 2.5 pounds (adjust the pricing to your location and supermarket). That is definitely cheaper than beef prices right now. How can you stretch fish when they are individually packaged?

Let me break it down for you: Slice lengthwise into strips and then slice again width-wise to make nuggets. oss it in some seasoned bread crumbs or cornmeal and either fry in a pan or oven bake. You will use less of these than you will if you gave someone an entire fillet for themselves and then you will probably pair it with vegetables and a salad or some homemade fries on the side. You can also use the filets to make a fish casserole, soup/bisque or chowder, or fish tacos where you would use much less for one person.

Canned tuna or tuna in a pouch is fabulous to make a casserole or tuna cakes with. It isn't just for tuna sandwiches anymore! You can often get them for very cheap and a little bit goes a long way. You can do the same with canned salmon or salmon in a pouch to get additional omega-3's in your diet since tuna shouldn't be consumed more than once a week or even twice due to the mercury content.

As you pass by all the meats, you stop to drool over a nice NY strip or a Ribeye. Stop salivating in the store, and pick up the least expensive one you can find. Yes, you can have it. Since you are not using one per person, you can make this one steak stretch in a way that will benefit your wallet and satisfy your desire for a delicious, melt-in-your-mouth steak. You can prepare the steak as you normally would and then slice it then and make fajitas out of them. Since you will be pairing it onions, peppers, and mushrooms, a little steak will go a long way. You can also slice the steak lengthwise and widthwise to use in quesadillas to be paired with a delicious salad. You can serve the steak over a bed of greens (think steak salad) or even seasoned rice. One steak can serve 1-3 people depending on the size of the steak and how you prepare it.

What about Italian sausage for the Italian dish lovers? You can't have Italian dishes without sausage, right? The best buy for the quality is at Costco. If all you can find is a package at your local grocery store, don't fret. I will show you how to make the most of that meat to feed your hungry family.

I generally use 3 sliced links (I slice it myself) in a crockpot with my homemade spaghetti sauce and let it continue to cook all day to allow the sausage to give my sauce some rich flavor. If I really want to make it stretch, I can take 2 links out of their casings, brown it in a skillet and add to the sauce. That will give you your sausage crumbles versus slices and allows you to use less. To add extra depth to your sauce, be sure to add tomatoes (even sun-dried tomatoes, onions, mushrooms, peppers, shredded carrots to sweeten, and fresh diced garlic (dried garlic is fine if that is what you have on hand). Adding the vegetables gives you a boost of nutrition, all while making your sauce chunkier since you are not adding additional meat. You can serve this over whole wheat pasta or even a nice, roasted spaghetti squash if you have gluten intolerances.

What about convenience meats such as already cubed stew meat or stir-fry meat? Am I against the concept of fresh meat all ready for me to cook? Absolutely not! When you find a great deal on meats that are already cut for specific meal types, saving the time in the kitchen chopping can be beneficial. When you purchase the cubed roast meat, dice them a little smaller and you can make a great vegetable beef soup, or a wonderful stew in the crockpot with potatoes, carrots and celery. If you find stir-fry meat on sale, you can turn that into fajitas (paired with grilled vegetables), quesadillas, enchiladas (paired with vegetables, cheese and beans) or even go Chinese and make Beef and Broccoli (paired with brown rice). The key is to find it reduced and then to pair it with "fillers" such as veggies and a complex starch to provide a meal for your family.

Part of our concept of meal time is to enjoy our foods. We were given taste buds for a reason and it can create wonderful emotions when eating something we enjoy. I don't want all of you to think that portioning your foods or trying to save money will result in cardboard tasting foods that cannot be enjoyable. Food is our medicine and our means of survival, but we can have "fun" preparing these meals while on the road to better health.

Chapter 6
Mooooove Over Milk, There's a New Sheriff In Town

THERE is a war raging on whether or not milk should even be in a human's diet at all, however this debate is not going to happen here. When we are focusing on a "good" diet, we are going to focus on the essentials needed to maintain health while shaving some dollars on the other end. So, raise your glass of milk and say "Cheers".

Since milk can be quite expensive at times depending on the brand and type purchased, it can really put a dent in your budget if allowed the opportunity. Because we have control over our finances and what we allow in our cart, we can outsmart the shrewdest businessman and still maintain our quality of life.

When my husband was heavy into weight-lifting, he drank a lot of protein shakes. As I would see our gallon of milk dwindle to nothing over the course of a few days, I gasped with anxiety knowing that our budget just didn't allow 5 gallons of milk a week. If you find yourself in this scenario or one that involves small children who love their milk, here's a hug for you. I feel your pain. While I love a great hug and pity party from time to time, there is no need to wallow in our sorrows over "spilled" milk in your cup.

We purchase dry milk as a staple in the home. It is vital to have it. Read that again. It is vital to have dry milk in your pantry. When the power goes out, the milk in your fridge will not last, but that milk in a canister or a box will carry on into the sunset. It is great for thickening soups, homemade yogurt, alfredo sauces and to make ...well, milk! It does have a distinct taste that some are not used to, so my battle plan to tackle this dilemma is to prepare half a pitcher with dry milk mixed with water and fill the rest with your favorite milk from the store. It will last longer and the flavor of the dry milk is undetectable.

When I am cooking, I generally have some prepared dry milk in my fridge to add to recipes instead of my "drinking" milk to allow it to stretch further. No one notices a difference, except my wallet, and sometimes that noisy and bossy, little thing has the loudest voice.

Milk is not the only thing we purchase from the dairy section, so let's tackle some other budget-busters while we are in this section. How about heavy whipping cream? Why should we consider this and should it make it into our grocery cart? It should if you are strapped to purchase butter, buttermilk or whipped cream. In one container of heavy whipping cream, you can get all 3 recipes at the same time. A bit confused? Let me clarify. Heavy whipping cream is what the farmers skim off the top of the milk. It is the richness that we love in all of our favorite alfredo recipes or potato soup. It ...is....amazing. Here is what you can do with it:

1. Place it in your food processor and whip until a yellow color develops. Continue processing until it is quite airy and choose if you want a whipped butter or a whipped cream. For whipped butter, add a bit of salt and process lightly. For whipped cream, add sugar. Voila! A whole lot of deliciousness that just cannot be contained! Spread your butter on your toast, bagels, or pancakes in the morning. The whipped cream is delicious on strawberry shortcake or on a fruit salad.

2. If you want solid butter, then continue to process in the food processor until the buttermilk separates from the solids. Take out your solid butter and put in a container in the fridge to use for all your favorite recipes.

3. The buttermilk run-off can be used to make homemade biscuits that will melt in your mouth.

Stroll with me down to the yogurt case and this place is filled with all sorts of brands that promise big benefits. The problem is, unless it is organic, it doesn't benefit your wallet or your health. So, what is a person to do when needing to get the most probiotics their money can buy? Make it yourself! It is so easy that my kids can do it themselves and for the yogurt incubators online, you can spend less than $20 for a decent one that will produce amazing results. You start off with a plain yogurt cup starter from the store, place it in a pot on the stove, grab one of the 6 jars your incubator holds and fill it up 6 times with milk of your choice. Stir the pot and heat until just warm, not hot, otherwise you will kill the bacteria and no yogurt will be created. If you like thicker yogurt, you can add 1 cup of dry milk to the pot and stir well. Then, ladle the mixture into the jars provided with the incubator, set it and forget it for roughly 12 hours and voila! Yogurt! It will be a bit sourer than what you will find in the store, but you can choose to sweeten it with some honey or make your own fruit topping for it. You can add a drop of vanilla extract or cinnamon for added flavor as well. The greatest part of this is you can use your own starter for your next yogurt batch.

Are you kind of bored with eating yogurt with a spoon? Here are some different ways to consume your yogurt and to rid yourself of the boredom that can result from the same ole', same ole'. You can add it to your smoothies for added protein and nutrition or you can make yogurt cheese. To make the cheese, place the yogurt into a cheesecloth and let it hang all day. Once in a while, when you walk by, give it a few squeezes and allow the whey to pour out into a bowl that you would store under the hanging yogurt. The whey can be used in your smoothie as it gives you the added protein benefit. After all the whey is out of the yogurt, you can scrape what is left into a bowl. It will have a cream cheese consistency and can be paired with herbs to use on your bagel or toast in the morning.

You can also add a touch of vanilla extract and coconut sugar or honey to it and make it a great dip with your tart fruits.

Now, let's talk about cottage cheese and how versatile it is. Despite the fact that you can make your own for minimal upfront costs, you can find a wonderful deal at the store from time to time. This cheese is freezable and able to be used in your lasagna in place of ricotta cheese and can also be blended up with some frozen raspberries and a bit of honey to sweeten for a nutritious snack. It can also be put into baked ziti and placed as a base for alfredo sauce. You can stock up when it is on sale, freeze it and prepare it once it is thawed in some of your favorite recipes....even bread!

What about the kids and their string cheese obsession? To save additional money from the pre-portioned cheese that you find in the supermarket, I would purchase a block of your favorite cheese and make the slices yourself. You can wrap them in plastic wrap and put them in a container in the fridge for an easy go-to snack. You can generally get more slices out of these than what you could purchase from your leading brands and it is real cheese. I really hate to be the bearer of bad news, but real cheese does not have strings. There, I said it. I feel better now, don't you?

Chapter 7
"Early to bed, early to rise, makes a man healthy, wealthy and wise"–Benjamin Franklin

BREAKFAST is super important to get into your day. Even if it is a piece of fruit, you need to break your fast from sleeping all night. You need to recharge or refuel your body from the lack of nutrients for those 8 hours of sleep the night before. While you were sleeping, your body was cleaning "house". All of the cells, muscles, and organs were being healed and cleaned from the day before. If you do not wake up and eat something, how do you think your body will muster up enough energy for the day and produce healthy cells?

Also, if your body runs off of protein, carbohydrates, fats, enzymes, amino acids, vitamins, minerals, water, and more, why would you put a sugary cereal in a bowl filled with milk in front of your children before they head to school? More and more kids are suffering from lack of concentration and the ability to focus. Their grades and the amount of prescription medications being dished out prove the case pretty solid. More children are growing more obese and are struggling with illnesses that most adults didn't expect to obtain until their "golden" years. This has become an absolute epidemic and it is something we have to change as parents in the home. Not only is it a health risk (as if that isn't enough), it is a costly one.

One box of cereal may last in a household for a few days, if we are lucky, and at $3 or more for a box of cereal, it isn't cost-effective in the long run. There are times that I will keep a few boxes of healthy cold cereal for the kids on hand, but for the most part, it is hot cereal that we invest in. Foods such as oatmeal, grits, and corn porridge are fabulous in the mornings. Not only do they "stick" with you longer than that cold cereal, but it is also loaded with nutrients that your body can actually assimilate versus running right through your systems like cold cereals. To make corn porridge, I use leftover cornbread from a night that I made chili (I freeze it until I need to use it) and one square represents one serving. I run it through my food processor after it is thawed (you can heat it in the microwave) until it crumbles. I transfer it to a pot with a pat of butter and enough milk to cover the crumbles. I don't add a sweetener if it is a sweet cornbread, but I do add cinnamon. I cook it until it is completely soft and like a porridge consistency. It is not only delicious, but it fills your kids up so that they are not hungry in an hour.

Some other breakfast ideas, but certainly not limited to are whole grain pancakes, eggs (boiled, fried, or scrambled), quiche, breakfast casserole, fruit and yogurt and breakfast burritos. When I make my own pancakes, I make a large enough batch for the entire month. I can make banana, strawberry, blueberry, and chocolate chip in different freezer bags and it is available in a flash when needed on the busy mornings. You can also make your own syrup by pureeing the fruits in a food processor and then transferring to a pot with a bit of water and sugar and let it cook until it gets syrupy. You may substitute stevia if needed. It is delicious over pancakes, waffles, French toast, or even your banana ice cream!

If your children are really throwing you some evil eyes over the cereal issue, then my suggestion would be to find the cereal with the least amount of sugar in it and sprinkle some wheat germ over the top to give some added nutrients to their food. Some habits die hard and as the parent, you have to find out what works best for you and improvise.

If your child is not really a breakfast person, here are some suggestions to make sure they get something in their tummy before you send them out to school. You can make muffins, give them a piece of fruit, a hard-boiled egg, homemade granola bar, toast with your yogurt cheese, and even a smoothie that is loaded with protein, vitamins, minerals and enzymes. There are times when drinking your meal is absolutely appropriate and if you are battling with a child, you have to weigh the cost: a screaming child prior to you having your coffee in the morning, or give them something that you know they will consume, is nutritious for them and you get peace and quiet at 7am. It's your call. I chose the latter with my kids.

The entire point is to recharge those batteries to give you the ultimate energy throughout your day. You only get one body and what you put into it is exactly what you are going to get out. If you don't put enough gasoline in your vehicle, you eventually will run out of gas and be stranded on the side of the road. Your body is much of the same. Don't leave yourself tired and weary mid-day. Put some high-octane fuel in your body aka vitamin and enzyme-rich foods that will help you perform at your very best.

Chapter 8
Pit Stop... Fuel and Go!

ALRIGHT, Nascar fans. This is your time to shine. On cue, how fast can you make a pit stop for lunch? You know how fast they work on those cars to keep them in tip-top shape, right? It is nothing short of a miracle to see the pristine nature of these vehicles once they are done. Just magnificent!

Think of your body the exact same way. We don't need to have a big lunch to fuel our bodies with the necessary vitamins, enzymes, and minerals it needs from each daily meal. Since our family prefers bigger breakfasts and bigger dinners due to my husband getting off of work around dinner-time, why have a large lunch and feel bloated and heavy all day long?

My solution is very simple! Get in and get out! Make yourself a wrap with your favorite healthy (reread that word…it says "healthy") food items that you can eat on the go or in just a few minutes. This is a meal that can be prepped the evening before and sitting in a container for the next day. You can use tuna, chicken, turkey bacon, turkey, ham or even boiled eggs! This doesn't have to be bland, but it does need to pack a powerful nutritional punch and sustain you until your next meal. You don't even need to purchase those expensive, super large wraps. You can use tortillas to keep the cost down as well. You generally get more for your money with those and it isn't overly large.

Another great way is to "drink" your lunch. You can make a delicious smoothie with kale, berries, carrots, or whatever you have in the fridge. You can add some yogurt or kefir for your probiotics, almond meal, flax meal, quinoa flour, PB2, wheat germ, wheat grass, protein, and milk (almond, cashew, cow's milk). This is a list of suggestions, not implied for you to add all of these into your smoothie at one time. If your smoothie is not sweet enough, throw in a banana to add a touch of sweetness or even a Medjool date.

The smoothie concept is great for moms on the go. I can't tell you how many times I have fed my kids and have forgotten to feed myself. This is my personal preference when my days are long and nights are short.

A grilled chicken salad is also a great nutritious lunch. You can add the veggies that need to be used in the fridge to top your salad and the best thing is that fruits and veggies are so rich in fiber that it helps sustain you until dinner time. I love to make boiled eggs and top a salad with it. It keeps my cost low all while giving me all the protein I truly need.

Soup is a wonderful and inexpensive alternative. You can make a huge pot of soup and have it ready in containers in the fridge for the entire week for lunch. Suggestions may include: Lentil, Split Pea, Ham and Bean, 15 Bean Soup, potato soup, Cream of Broccoli (or celery and mushroom), homemade Tomato Soup, Chicken Noodle etc. I am so guilty of becoming overzealous of my produce shopping. Can you blame me? They are so amazing for us and the sales and deals scream my name. However, after my "hoarding" tendencies subside, I see all these items that need to get used or there is a waste that develops. This is truly where my "souping" has taken off. I have found that I can make delicious soups using these vegetables to help offset waste, all while filling up with broth and nutritious vegetables. Win, win! If you truly know me, you will know that I love to win…it is the competitive nature in me. Whether it is a game of "Risk" or creating a masterpiece in the kitchen that keeps the cost down, it is all the same to me. No judging.

The most important point I want to convey to you is that you can be totally creative in this department and have enjoyable meals. I don't eat cardboard. I eat delicious food every single day! You can too!

Chapter 9
Multiplying the Savings to Infinity and Beyond!

W HEN the money gets a bit tighter around our home, the meals tend to get smaller. I hope I am reaching someone that knows the feeling and that I am not the only one out of 7 billion people that can relate to this. How do we remedy this situation and continue to put money in our bank? Let me show some simple ways.

Once a week, my family and I eat a "panini" (fancy name for a sandwich on regular bread that has been grilled on my George Foreman grill) and some soup (using whatever vegetables I have on hand). My husband is an avid runner and works hard all day. He does not leave my table feeling hungry. The soup is a wonderful complement to the sandwich and has filled my family up for years. I make homemade tomato soup with our grilled ham, cheese and spinach sandwiches or even on those cold, winter nights here in Colorado, we indulge in a potato soup with a dash of dill. Here are some soup ideas that aim to satisfy:

* Potato Soup: Can be topped with bacon, green onions, or a sprinkle of cheese

* Broccoli and Cheese Soup: Can be topped with Pico de Gallo

* Cream of Broccoli, Celery, Mushroom or Spinach Soup

* Homemade Cream of Tomato Soup

* French Onion Soup: Served with a slice of toast cut in half and provolone cheese melted over it

* Lentil Soup: Served with bacon crumbles
* Split Pea Soup: Topped with ham crumbles (use a food processor to make the crumbles)
* Chicken Noodle Soup
* Cream of spinach Soup
* Vegetable Beef Soup
* Minestrone
* Pasta Fagioli
* Zuppa Toscana

By looking at the list above, you are able to see that our soups are not bland or tasteless meals. Why should food be bland and boring? None of us would stick to any budget if it consisted of foods that failed to satisfy. By keeping the flavors in the meal and becoming creative in this endeavor, it can help us to not miss the over-priced and chemical-laden foods that we discover out on the town.

For those of you that are not into the whole "soup and sandwich" idea, I have others that may strike your fancy! Breakfast is not just for the A.M. anymore. Have you heard the latest news? You can now "officially" eat eggs for...wait for it, DINNER. I realize that this is not exactly new news, but too many have not fully taken advantage of this excellent opportunity to save money by introducing this to the family. Shocker, I know. You can make anything from omelets, fried eggs, boiled eggs, quiche, frittatas, scrambled, breakfast burritos, breakfast casseroles, or even egg sandwiches. How can you have "fried" rice without a scrambled egg? To do so would be a crime. It gives the rice so much depth and flavor and is a meal you can have on the table in less than 30 minutes. Egg is a wonderful protein (as long as one is not allergic) that is extremely affordable. It really helps to offset the cost of beef, chicken, and pork.

Sam's club has 15 dozen eggs for under $20.00 at our location. Can you just imagine the possibilities?

Do you have leftovers you've forgotten in the fridge that have the potential to be a science experiment? Let's eradicate this problem, pronto. When we do not use the foods that we have already cooked we are wasting more dollars. Maybe you cooked too much the last few nights and just were not feeling like having them again and again. You don't have to!

When we have leftovers, you can portion the food and freeze them in containers
or Ziploc® bags. This removes the waste issue and your boredom at the same time. Even if there is only one serving leftover, I freeze it anyway. When I have 5 or 6 items in my freezer taking up space, I pull them all out and have a "free for all" night. It is a way for me to squeeze one more meal out of what we have and the kids are always happy since there is something that everyone likes in the batch.

Another way you can utilize your leftovers is to turn it into soup or a casserole.

Both of these menu categories utilize meat, veggies and a starch. There are plenty of recipes you can find where you can incorporate these items to squeeze another meal. A friend mentioned to me how her mother always had a bowl that she would add to in the freezer filled with meat and veggies. When the bowl was completely full, she made soup!

Who says that meat has to be a staple in every meal anyway? Why not try a vegetarian meal once or twice a week to give your body and your wallet a break? Meat takes the longest for your body to digest out of all the food groups; digesting at a rate of 5-6 hours. Fruit takes approximately 15-20 minutes to digest. Vegetables digest roughly in an hour. Carbohydrates take an estimated 2 hours. A system overloaded with animal proteins can wreak havoc on your body. Not to mention, our budgets can use a little relief as well. Here are some ideas for you:
   * Vegetable Lasagna with a salad
   *Macaroni and Cheese with a side of broccoli
   * Veggie burgers with homemade potato wedges
   *Beans and brown rice
   *Meatless Chili
   *Veggie Fajitas

The list can go on and on, but I wanted to give you an idea that many times we are programmed to think that we need meat, starch, vegetable, fruit and milk at every meal. I am here to tell you that, there are many ways you can eat meat-free a couple of times a week that do not stress the budget, improves your overall health, and can taste amazing! Be a rebel, go ahead.

At times, our home can seem like a prison to us. In efforts to save money, we often neglect going out and enjoying life. This can mean that restaurants are not on our list of entertainment options. I can agree that going out all the time to paint the town red is never a good idea when one is on a budget. Nor is it a great idea for our waistlines.

We spend countless dollars on food that is often made with poor quality and is marked up way beyond it's worth. Then, we tip 15-20% (At least everyone should tip this much as the server only makes $2.13 an hour. They depend on that income to pay out the bar, hostesses, busboys, and to live off of.) For my family of four, we could spend anywhere from $40-100 per meal out. That is nearly my budget for a couple weeks to almost a month! So, when we want to eat out as a treat, we tend to skip the steakhouses and go for the places that offer our kids to eat free on certain days. You can often do a google search for restaurants in your area that offer these deals. We save by not having the added expense of their meals and we get to have an enjoyable night out every so often.

We also promote water-drinking at the table to save additional costs. Not only is water best for you, but it is FREE. Go back and read that again. I know you liked that word...FREE. Each soft drink purchased is at $1.50. For our family of four, it is $6.00 right off the bat and we haven't ordered anything. We also have chosen to not purchase any appetizers if we are getting a meal. We often do not finish our meal when getting an appetizer and it is an unnecessary expense. Several restaurants still serve free rolls or chips before your meal comes out. Voila! Happy free appetizer!

When selecting a meal off of the menu, here are some money-saving pointers that can be useful:

*If you want a salad, order a side salad. It is way cheaper than those advertised, is portioned exactly as you need and you can purchase one for less than $5 at most places.

* Look for meals large enough for you to share. Some of those portions are just too large for one person to eat in one sitting. Many restaurants will split the meal for you on two separate plates as well. The only time you are not able to do this is if it is an "all you can eat" situation. No sharing or take outs are allowed.

*Order side dishes of your favorite veggies for less than what an entree may cost you. You are still eating much better than if you ordered that bacon cheeseburger, and saving in the process–more ways than one.

*Order an appetizer as your meal. Most people are no longer hungry after an appetizer. There may be "room" for more, but the actual feeling of hunger subsides when food enters the stomach. The portions are smaller and usually leave you content without feeling stuffed, full and tired.

*Do not purchase dessert at the restaurant. I know I just beat you while you were already down. I mean, LOOK at that double chocolate fudge brownie loaded with vanilla ice cream and hot fudge topped with walnuts! Let me hand you a napkin to wipe the drool from your lips running down your chin and offer you some advice. Most desserts cost $5 on up. Multiply that amount by how many desserts you will need to purchase for each person and that is just insanity. I understand that you could share that dessert with each person at the table, but do you realize that is entering a battleground? At least for our family, we would be fighting to the death to get the last bite. Many fingers have been sacrificed by spoons for the sake of what should have been a loving and caring event. Sharing is caring, right? Let me offer a better option.

*I am, by no means, an advocate for fast food chains, but getting a dollar sundae for EACH person is less than $5 and better than fighting with the people I love so dearly. I really want to keep it that way. On occasion, our family will do this as a nice treat. Life is to be enjoyed, right? Remember that on occasion these things are not going to be a big deal in the big scheme of things, but if we do it all the time in the name of celebration, you are well on your way to many health issues.

*You can also make dessert prior to leaving to go to the restaurant and have it ready upon your return home. It is much cheaper and saves your bill. The ingredients are better for you as well.

Some of you may be reading this and thinking, "I just can't afford to go out at all. This just isn't h elpful." Let me encourage you for a minute. I have been in hard times where my family and I can relate. I took it upon myself to learn how to make the foods that I loved going to restaurants to eat. For instance, I love Chinese. I do not even believe that "love" is a strong enough word for the type of commitment I have for this type of food. However, I do know that I can make it at home for cheaper, healthier and much quicker than I can order the takeout and for it to be delivered. I found amazing recipes online on how to make my own Beef and Broccoli and Szechuan Chicken. I have been told that my Szechuan Chicken tastes just like the buffets! What a wonderful compliment!

Many of the restaurants post recipes on their websites. I have found delicious recipes from Olive Garden, Red Lobster, and many other restaurants. They a re u sually t he r ecipes t hat h ave been phased out from the menu, but to us, it is GOLD. For their famous recipes, you can find "copycats" all over the internet for free.

A way to make this more fun and entertaining is to put the recipes from the restaurant in a hat or a bowl and each time you are wanting a special treat, have a different p erson p ick a recipe out. To step this up a notch, we have even used the nationality of food that we chose as a time for extra learning. If we are eating Chinese food, we may learn about the Chinese culture. If we are eating Italian, we can learn about Italy. Mealtimes don't have to be boring. You can create your own entertainment in the house all while enjoying a meal that you prepared at home for more than likely less than $10. There is always a solution, which gives each of us hope.

Chapter 10
"Houston, we have a problem..." – Emergency Preparedness

OVER the course of several years, I have seen more and more people prep for "Doomsday". There was even a show on called "Doomsday Preppers" where they were so prepared for disaster to strike that they had to also set up a defense to guard and protect it. In case you think I am going to send you to the store to buy the finest of tin foil to make your hats, let me first say, fear has no place here. This chapter will not be devoted to fear, but to wisdom in the harshest conditions.

In America, we have so much privilege that often times it can blind us from the reality at hand. We cannot control the weather. We cannot speak to the hurricanes, earthquakes, tornadoes and other natural disasters and ask it to please get out of our backyard. They will strike at any time. Are you prepared?

Hurricane Katrina left so many people devastated. People were without homes, food, clean drinking water, and a way out of the nightmare that encased them. If this were you, would you have a plan for your current situation? Do you have a stockpile of food that does not need to be refrigerated or frozen to survive on? Most people do not.

In the event disaster strikes, my hope is to not only be able to feed my family, but also others that do not have anything. So, please understand that this chapter is not geared towards, "Let me hoard", but rather, "Prepare to give." Even if disaster never strikes, hard times come and go. Storing up for those times is considered an investment.

We discussed canning in an earlier chapter, but it is worth mentioning again. This technique for food storage is paramount. Foods can last so very long with this method and it is easy once you learn how to do it. I recommend learning how to water bath can first before going to pressure canning. Water bath canning is for acidic foods only, so no low-acid foods such as vegetables or meats can be canned this way.

Some things I can currently are chilies, salsa, spaghetti sauce, jam, pie fillings, and homemade pancake syrup. Pinterest has so many recipes and ideas for you to help create the stockpile. The mason jars are costly, but the replacement lids and rings are inexpensive to replace. The jars can be reused unless you find cracks or weak points in the glass.

It can be very overwhelming when first trying to prepare your foods, so my suggestion is to pick one food a month that you want to can. Purchase the size jars you need, find the recipe you want to try and make as many as you can. By the end of the year, you will have a nice stock of those items.

Dehydrating food is also a great way to keep foods from spoiling. Make sure that you find a dehydrator that contains settings for the different types of food that you may want to dehydrate. I purchased mine for $60.00 and it is wonderful. Here's a small list of things that you can prepare to dehydrate:
* Fruit leather or roll ups
* Dried milk
*Sour cream powder
*Instant potato flakes
*Dried eggs (can be used for scrambled eggs or omelets)
*Spices from dried herbs
* Soup mixes
*Spaghetti with sauce and meat
*Cooked beans

*Jerky
*Breadcrumbs
*Stuffing/Dressing
*Croutons
*Cheese
*Au gratin potatoes

This list can go on through infinity. It is great to have deep freezers to store your foods. It is great to have canned goods, but to have dehydrated foods in your storage is ESSENTIAL. Not only do they not take up space, but they are easy to rehydrate. You should always weigh your food prior to dehydrating. Once it is done in the dehydrator, weigh your food again. The amount of weight lost is how much in water you will need to rehydrate the food. There are so many recipes online and Youtube videos to show you exactly how to do this, it is virtually foolproof.

Not only is this device a miracle worker to shrink the food's weight (Disclaimer: Please do not attempt on yourself), but it is also a time-saver. Once you place the food into the dehydrator, you leave it alone for hours on end and let it do its job. Not much fuss, but we reap the rewards.

Want an Emergency Preparedness Survival Guide to Appliances? Look no further. Although I absolutely believe in other appliances, these are essential to prepping:

*Dehydrator
*Canner
*Solar-powered grill or oven (when power goes out)
*Cast iron pans to cook on your stove, in your oven or on an open fire (not an appliance, but still essential)
*Food processor
*Coffee grinder (helps better to prepare the dried milk, potatoes, and eggs into a fine powder)

For those of you who are overzealous and excited about prepping, you can always learn how to hunt your own game and learn how to fish. This would bring in a ton of free food for you. You can dehydrate it or pressure can it for emergencies. This is a skill that our family is hoping to learn just because it absolutely makes sense. The food is free (other than the license to hunt and the cost of the weapon), the family learns survival skills and, often, a butcher will process your meat for a portion of the meat to resell. It is a win-win for all.

If hunting for your own food is not appealing to you, please let me suggest other venues for you to obtain your food to receive the best deals.

Zaycon Foods is a company that I trust. They are not organic, but every bit of all-natural. There are no antibiotics or hormones in the food, no tax or delivery charge and it is straight from the farm to you. You are able to order by the case and order as many as you would like and it is much cheaper than purchasing from a grocery store. This company also allows you to earn Zaycon dollars in your account by volunteering at their "events" and by referring others to their wonderful company. Also, if you order a case of meat and the weight is not as advertised, they will refund you the difference automatically in your Zaycon account. That can be used for future purchases or you can have it transferred into your bank account. Talk about an honest company! You can find them here: https:"zayconfresh.com/refer/zf339263.

I want to also include in this chapter that by taking your income tax and setting aside a portion dedicated to food for the year is so helpful. This also allows me to purchase better and healthier choices since we receive a decent chunk back every year. We purchase our meat and dry storage items around this time to alleviate the burden of each and every month having to spend $200 for our family of four. We actually spend about $100 a month on fresh fruits and veggies and our essentials by doing it this way. It also limits the amount of grocery trips I tackle in a month, which means more savings in our wallet from impulse buying.

In order to do this, a deep freezer would be a must. Deep Freezers are worth their weight in gold. When you are prepping, making food every night and stocking up during sales, you need a place to store all your food. You can usually find them used by searching yard sale sites such as Craigslist or Bookoo. If you live near a military base, look for PCS sales. You would be amazed at the deals you can find there

Chapter 11
Whistle While You Work...."

SINCE food is not the only item we purchase at the supermarket, let me also include cleaning products. When I walk down the cleaning aisle, I am faced with all the detergents that promise me the world in exchange for my first born. It is ridiculous how expensive cleaning agents are these days and it is like they know we are going to need them every month and when we run out, (gasp), we will have to repurchase. These marketing stalkers creep into our homes and tiptoe into our lives looking for ways to separate us from our money. What if I told you that you clean better, and more effectively without their products?

How can we improve on nature? We are finding in all areas of science that what is natural is the best for us than what is not. Of course, this makes sense since we are "natural" beings. All the fragrance and chemicals that go into those products are toxins to us. They wreak havoc on our health and for our pets as well. Here are some tried and true cleaners that are inexpensive to make while completely cleaning your home efficiently and effectively:

Vinegar and water is a deodorizer and a multipurpose cleaner. It disinfects and for 2 gallons at Sam's Club, it is less than $4. You can mix essential oils into the solution, but it is not necessary to be effective.

*Vinegar and baking soda is a powerful degreaser.

*Hydrogen Peroxide whitens and also gets blood stains out of clothes.

*Laundry soap can be made with Ivory soap (grated), borax, and washing soda.

*You can add OxiClean™ if you want extra cleaning power. Mix well and put in a bucket.

*There is a magnetic laundry system that uses magnets to change the surface tension of the water. This cleans the clothes without chemicals or added ingredients. It is a one-time purchase and is completely refundable. They have a lifetime guarantee on it as well. It is called "MLS"–Magnetic Laundry System.

*Rubbing alcohol cleans microfiber couches.

*Vinegar cleans mirrors without streaks.

*Lemon juice mixed in cooking oil cleans wood furniture.

*Baking soda and salt can clean tubs.

*Baking soda mixed with essential oils is a great air freshener

After cleaning products, personal hygiene is also increasing in cost yearly. I advocate making your own products versus purchasing due to the chemical overload our bodies take in and also the price tag doesn't do me any favors. I make my own deodorant, body wash, and toothpaste myself. Here are some ideas for you:

* Take a bar of soap of your choice (I use Ivory. You will need 8 oz) and grate it. Place in a large bowl and add some coconut oil, olive oil or avocado oil. The amount is completely up to you. Pour boiling hot water over the soap mixture and use an immersion blender to blend well. Let it sit overnight and give it another blend in the morning. Pour into plastic containers and use the same as normal body wash. The consistency can be a little off for some people, but I use it all the time. It makes my skin super soft and clean and the savings speaks volumes. I get plastic bottles for body wash from Amazon and fill them up. You can add essential oils, Vitamin E, or anything else you would like.

*Your own deodorant does not have to be difficult. There are many ways to make it, but to make it the cheapest, I use coconut oil and baking soda. I mix well and then add it to empty and clean deodorant containers. Sometimes the baking soda can create a darkening under the arms. If that happens, you can switch to arrowroot powder in place of the baking soda. Due to the coconut oil, the deodorant will need to be refrigerated. I apply once in the morning and do not need to reapply until the next day. You can also add essential oils if you would like, but again, it is not necessary. The benefit of this deodorant is that it does not stain your clothes, the baking soda neutralizes odor and coconut oil has antibacterial properties while soothing the skin.

*Just like deodorant, toothpaste recipes abound much, so if this recipe doesn't suit your taste, then by all means find one online. I personally use turmeric, cinnamon, baking soda, and coconut oil for my toothpaste. It is an acquired taste, but I like the end results. It has to be refrigerated due to the coconut oil, but the turmeric is great for inflammation, cinnamon is antibacterial and helps with blood circulation, and the baking soda cleans. You can make this minty-fresh as well with essential oils. If you are used to mainstream toothpaste, this will definitely be a change for you. Just know that you will get used toit and your gums and enamel will thank you.

These are just a few items for you to start with, but hopefully will ignite the passion for diving into more self-care items for you and your family. Some items are inevitable and will have to be purchased, but you can offset the cost by limiting how much you really purchase and how often. Anytime we can put extra funds back into our pockets to put into savings, get out of debt and make positive sustainable changes in our lives, the better our well-being.

Chapter 12
"Change Starts With You..."

Too often we sit back and ponder the rising costs of groceries, fuel, bills, clothes, and all of our necessities. Does it take time and effort to be intentional about saving money? Sure, it does. Anything worth working towards takes some effort. We will always make time for what is truly important to us. If the high balance of our credit card is stopping us from getting our lives onto a healthy track, then remove the obstacle that is creating the issue one step at a time.

This approach works for all social classes, all incomes, and all lifestyles. Some of you may be stay at home mothers, so you may be able to prepare more throughout your day than someone that may work a full-time job or have two jobs. For those of you who have limited time, make one new item a week. Here is a suggested schedule to inspire you to brainstorm some ideas:

Week 1— Muffins

Week 2—Pancakes

Week 3—Bean and Cheese Burritos

Week 4– Breakfast burritos

Week 5–Jam

Week 6–Spaghetti sauce

Week 7– Frozen pizzas

Week 8–Ready-made meals

Week 9–Portioning of meats

Week 10–Make bread rolls for sandwiches (you can freeze these for future use).

This is merely a suggestion to show you that Rome was not built in a day (nor was it destroyed in a day either) and neither will your stockpile. Do one thing at a time until you see the pantry stocked up with essentials that you need. It truly does work for any lifestyle.

I run two businesses, homeschool my children, and go to school myself. I still have to chauffeur my children around to all their activities as well. If I can find time to work towards sustainability, I truly believe you can as well. Saving money in this way is working towards a pathway to freedom. With every bill that gets paid off, you can feel the load lessen, and the burdens fade away. There is power in being debt-free and not owing a penny to anyone. No one will be looking over your shoulder. No one will be calling your phone. All the extra cash flow can go to bettering your healthy eating choices, savings, and helping others in your community. Why is this natural health practitioner so concerned about your finances? You caught me again. I have an ulterior motive.

In my training, we have learned so much about what creates a life filled with disorders, disease, and even life-threatening situations. We know that our body has three main components: mind, body, and spirit. If one of these is imbalanced, it throws the other two off as well. One of the primary stressors I have heard from many people is financial burden. "I would purchase organic if I could afford it!" or "I can't eat healthy or purchase those supplements I need for support because I just don't have the money to spend." There are times when people could actually prioritize what is important to them and not purchase coffee or something at a fast food chain, but I know the majority of you honestly cannot find relief. If I can help you by saving you hundreds of dollars each month on groceries, while becoming self-reliant and sustainable, I know it will create a spark that will ignite a passion for you to take care of your bills. Once the hindrances are gone, your health will improve, your quality of life improves and then we can start taking you from the "Good" diet and moving you to a "Better diet," which will set you up for the "Best" diet for you. I know, I know. I am a sneaky one. However, the only one that truly benefits from making these changes is you.

I learned these tricks from real-life experiences. My husband and I went through very tough times, and it was in those times that I learned the power of being frugal. You have to believe that you are worth more than what your credit report reveals. You are worth more than what a debt-collector perceives you as (they can be downright nasty). You owe it to yourself to be sustainable and self-reliant. You deserve to invest in yourself and not be a slave to the lenders. Don't buy into the lie that the life you are living is what was planned out for you. There are always ways to change your outcome, but the change always starts with you.

Chapter 13
Additional Ways to Get Out of Debt Quickly

Listed below, I have provided some of the main appliances I use in the order of necessity. I started off with a small food processor, and as we did better financially, I was able to replace it with a much larger one with attachments. If you are unable to purchase these appliances, please do not despair! You can follow the steps and guidelines in the book to the extent you are able, and as money is freed up in your check, you can start looking into additional ways that can help you expand and save. Keep in mind that this is an investment and it will pay for itself repeatedly. The key is to start where you can (even with a small fridge freezer and storage bags) and find those deals when you can afford them. I started with a small refrigerator freezer. I began portioning my meat since that was the most expensive item to purchase. I branched out over time with bean and cheese burritos and more. So be encouraged!
   * Food Processor
   * Deep Freezer
   *Slow Cooker
   *Food Saver®
   *Canner
   * Dehydrator
   *Yogurt Maker
   *Immersion Blender
   *Blender
   *Griddle

*Coffee Grinder
*Pasta Maker

If you are just starting out, it can be overwhelming to have a fully-stocked kitchen filled with all of these appliances. My suggestion is to ask for some of these items as Christmas or birthday presents from family instead of things you do not need. I personally just requested a gift card where I could combine the funds to purchase what was needed.

Another option is to look on Amazon, eBay or thrift stores to find discounted and used items that are still in terrific condition. Yard sale sites and garage sales can significantly help keep funds in the bank. I also find thriftier brands of vacuum seal bags for my FoodSaver® on Amazon than if I was to purchase them at a department store. You know what your budget is, so be sure to stick to it. Deals come around all the time, so if you miss it once, you will see it again.

If you find that the creativity train has left the station in your time of need, Pinterest is a great option. I mention it throughout this book because it has saved me so much time trying to navigate different sites that may have popped up on Google. I often do not share recipes as I rarely measure when I cook. This makes it difficult for others to replicate. It is much easier for me to give you ideas so that you may search for what works for your family in a venue that has so much more to offer you.

If you are seeking to get out of debt very quickly, here are some other ways to consider saving money and some things to research. Please note that I am by no means a financial advisor, but have found relief by these methods that I wish to share with all of you:

*Contact your internet company and see if they offer a loyalty discount

*Cut cable and purchase rabbit ears for your TV. Rabbit ears have advanced since when I was a child. Now, you have a lot more channels to choose from, and it is crystal clear. Because it is a one-time purchase, you save the monthly cable bill. Most of us pay for channels we just don't use through cable. Rabbit ears allow for you

to get all your local channels and most sports at no monthly cost to you.

*Consider Netflix, Hulu, Sling, Pure Flix and the like for a small monthly fee if you truly miss your TV shows. Many of the new episodes will soon be on these streaming sites right after the season is over. If you must watch it as it airs, consider Sling. Sling also allows for those football games to stream that you cannot get on rabbit ears (ESPN).

*Look into other cell phone companies that may be cheaper than your existing provider. Such companies as MetroPCS, Republic Wireless, Ting and for those that qualify there is the Lifeline Assistance Program, which is a free benefit. We often pay for services that we either do not need or do not use that can put a serious dent in our wallet. Look to minimize these areas.

*Check into cheaper car insurance from such companies like Esurance®. You often get better coverage while saving money. If it is not available in your area, still search the companies that reside in your location to see if they have competitive rates.

*Use your income tax refund to purchase food for the year, pay small bills up for the year, and to pay off any debt you may have. For many, this lump sum money can seriously help tackle your monthly services such as internet, Netflix, car insurance, pest control, trash services, water, gas, gym memberships, HOA dues, and more. All those little bills that can eat up your paycheck that you need, pay them up with that lump sum to alleviate the stress from your month. Be sure to allocate money to your savings as well.

*If you homeschool, please take advantage of my Facebook group called "Homeschooling on a Dime". I post a lot of free resources and often complete curricula to help curb the burden of homeschooling. This is mentioned here due to the rise in homeschooling families.

*Switch to Magic Jack for your home service to help keep your cellular usage down. It costs us $99 for 5 years and allows us to use our cell phones less. We have switched to smaller cellular plans because it is no longer needed as often as it was before.

*Re-grow food from scraps! Foods like celery, cabbage, lettuce, green onions and more will regrow if placed in water. Once they start growing again, replant them into pots to get the nourishment they need. I also like to keep at least one potato to "spud". One potato has many "eyes" on it. Each eye has the potential to grow another plant that can produce up to 8 other potatoes!

*Save the seeds from your produce to grow your own food at home.

*Don't pay the high prices at the movie theaters. Wait for the movie to come out on Redbox and pay $1.60 versus $30.00 for the movie ticket, popcorn, drink, etc. If you are treating yourself to the movies on occasion, take advantage of matinee or discounted pricing. If you are a student, military, or a senior citizen, they are often c heaper. The Carmike theaters have an annual bucket that you purchase that allows you to receive refills of popcorn each time you come in for only $4. It is enough to feed my family of four and then some! We usually attend a movie for special occasions or as a reward for the kids for doing well in school. We do not make it a regular practice.

*We take advantage of free events for the entire family that are happening locally. If you live in a small town that often does not have ongoing activities, be creative and create your own activity. You can pack for a picnic, play sports with your kids, build forts in the house, do art projects, play board games and so much more. Not having cash flow should never stop someone from enjoying life. We often have made the best memories with our family with NO money.

We sometimes believe that life will officially be gin wh en we make "more" money. That isn't always the c ase. The answer isn't always "more", but to learn to budget what you already have. Promotions are wonderful, more cash flow seems to please us for a while, but if our habits do not change, we will be stuck in the same rut–more bills and living above our means. If we change the habits now, when we do get that promotion that we are looking so forward to, we would make wiser choices with the money that is given to us.

If we also do not make it a regular practice to give to others and be generous, we can find that our money takes control over us. Dave Ramsey, a financial adviser and creator of "Financial Peace University", goes into depth about how our hearts are when we have little money is very telling to how they will be when we have lots of it. You can often find churches offering this class of his for free. I highly recommend taking it to take charge of your overall financial well-being.

Believe in your worth. Invest in your future. Small steps equal enormous benefits.

About the Author

Jessica Cassidy resides in Colorado with her wonderful husband, Jon, and two amazing children, Jonathan, and Jesslynn. She is a Certified Natural Health Professional, Certified Health Specialist, speaker, and continues to teach on natural health. She is currently attending school to achieve her Doctorate of Natural Health and hopes to fulfill her passion of helping others find healing through the foods they eat and lifestyle changes. She volunteers to help the homeless in her community and looks for opportunities to combine natural health and budget counseling to help the impoverished community.

www.ingramcontent.com/pod-product-compliance
Lightning Source LLC
Chambersburg PA
CBHW060631280326
41933CB00012B/2005